For Evan and Michael, who gave me the idea.
—AR

To Mason and Reuben.
—SB

Published by Sourcebooks eXplore, an imprint of Sourcebooks Kids
P.O. Box 4410, Naperville, Illinois 60567-4410
(630) 961-3900
sourcebookskids.com
Cataloging-in-Publication Data is on file with the Library of Congress.
Source of Production: Wing King Tong Paper Products Co. Ltd., Shenzhen, Guangdong Province, China
Date of Production: March 2023
Run Number: 5030558
Printed and bound in China.
WKT 10 9 8 7 6 5 4 3 2 1

ANIMAL SNUGGLES

AFFECTION IN THE ANIMAL KINGDOM

Words by Aimee Reid

Pictures by Sebastien Braun

sourcebooks
eXplore

Belly to belly.

Sea otter mothers float on their backs and
carry their babies on their bellies.

Cheek to cheek.

Horses nuzzle to say hello or show
that they like one another.

Elbow to elbow.

Because of their short arms, when a mother and baby kangaroo hug, their elbows come close together.

Beak to beak.

Parent swans lean in close to
call gently to their babies.

In the hot desert,
nose to nose.

Rabbits touch noses to bond with
each other and to make peace.

On a cold snow drift,
toes to toes.

Emperor penguin fathers hold their
newborn chicks in a special pouch by their feet.

Down in a burrow,
safe and snug.

Puffin parents care for their puffling in a cozy spot underground.

High on a mountain,
in a hug.

Mama bears snuggle
with their cubs to
warm and feed them.

Through the thick jungle,
side by side.

The mother tiger is the main caretaker
of her cubs, so she stays very
close to keep them safe.

On the savannah,
with the pride.

A lioness builds a special den to care for her newborn cubs—just her and them.

Under the ocean.

On the trail.

Flipper to flipper.

A dolphin mother swims close to her baby
to help it move through the water more easily.

Trunk to tail.

Baby elephants can use their trunks
to hold their mother's tail.

Shoulder to shoulder.

Knee to knee.

Animals cuddle.
So do we.

Chimpanzees love
to groom each other,
snuggle, and hug.

Nothing is sweeter.
Nothing more true.

Heartbeat to
heartbeat.

Me with you.

SNUGGLY ANIMALS

SEA OTTERS

A baby sea otter, called a pup, is born with fur that helps it to float in water. A pup can't swim until it is about four weeks old, though, so it nestles on its mother's belly to ride along while she swims on her back. When the mom needs to look for food, she can wrap kelp around her pup so that it doesn't float away.

HORSES

A mother horse is called a mare. Her baby horse is called a foal. Mares and foals often make soft, low sounds to one another. This is called nickering. Mares and foals touch cheeks and nuzzle each other with their noses to breathe in one another's familiar scent.

KANGAROOS

Baby kangaroos are called joeys. A joey stays in a special pouch on its mother's belly where it feeds and snuggles. When it is about eight months old, a joey begins to leave the pouch for a little while. A mama kangaroo will make a special clucking sound to call her joey back to her. When a joey wants to go back inside the pouch, it can pop in headfirst and do a somersault so that its head peeks back out of the pouch.

SWANS

A mother swan is called a pen, and a father swan is called a cob. The baby is a cygnet. The pen and cob make special sounds so that their cygnets will recognize them. Each swan makes a unique sound. To help their babies hear them, the pen and cob often bring their faces very close to the cygnets.

RABBITS

A mother rabbit makes a nest for her babies with grass and adds fur that she pulls from her belly. When her babies, called kits, are born, they are only about two inches long. Kits begin to hear and see when they are around ten days old, and they depend on their mothers for milk. Rabbits may sit peacefully with noses touching for quite a long time.

EMPEROR PENGUINS

After an emperor penguin mother lays an egg, she goes out to sea to fish. The father then cares for the egg without eating for the two months the mother is away! The father keeps the egg on his feet and covers it with special feathered skin called a brood pouch. Emperor penguins often huddle together to stay warm. They live in large colonies, but each chick has a unique call that its parents recognize.

PUFFINS

Puffins dig burrows about as long as a grown human's arm and build a soft nest inside. Puffin babies are called pufflings, and puffin parents usually have one puffling at a time. The puffling's fluffy down feathers help keep it warm when a parent goes to catch fish. The mother and father both help raise the baby. Puffin parents feed their pufflings multiple times a day. They have special beaks that let them catch and carry several fish at once—up to about ten!

BLACK BEARS

Baby black bears are born in dens in the wintertime. The babies, called cubs, need their moms to feed them and keep them warm and safe. Cubs and mothers stay close, with new cubs cuddling up to their moms to sleep. As the cubs get bigger, they may enjoy a ride on their mother's back. A mother bear sometimes sits and holds her babies within her front legs while she grooms and nurses them.

TIGERS

When tiger cubs are born, they are blind. Their eyes open after about six to twelve days. A mother tiger is very careful to protect her babies. She will move them if she thinks they need to be hidden in another spot, carrying them by gently holding the backs of their necks with her teeth! A tiger mom spends a lot of time licking her babies' fur, and each tiger's striped pattern is different.

LIONS

A lioness makes a special hidden den where she will give birth to her babies. She looks for places like thick grass, deep woods, or high rocks, and she may move the babies a few times a month until they are bigger. Lion cubs begin to crawl about a day or two after birth, and they walk when they are about three weeks old. A lioness stays alone with her cubs until the babies are about six to eight weeks old.

DOLPHINS

Baby dolphins are called calves. They live with their mothers and other dolphins in pods. Dolphin calves stay safe in the middle of the pod. A mother dolphin swims just above and to the side of her young calf. As the water flows around the mother, it helps pull the baby along, making it easier for the child to keep up. The mother dolphin may rub her flipper along her baby as they swim together.

ELEPHANTS

When a mother elephant is having a baby, the other female elephants in her herd often gather around and make loud trumpeting sounds. Aunties, sisters, and cousins help to care for the baby as it grows. They use their trunks to greet, soothe, and guide the young elephant. When walking with her baby, a mother often touches it with her trunk or tail. To show it wants to rest, a calf might press against its mother's front legs.

CHIMPANZEES

Chimpanzees live in groups of about twenty to thirty and include members from a few generations. These chimps eat and play together and teach the little members of the group important skills. Grown males will often play with the young chimps. Chimpanzees touch each other a lot: They groom each other as a way of connecting and hug to say hello.

Aimee Reid is a children's book author with a background in editing and teaching English, music, and special education. As a child, Aimee was a voracious reader, and today she loves sending her own stories into the world. Aimee lives in Canada, where she enjoys reading, writing, and snuggling with her loved ones, including her sweet dog, Sadie.

Sébastien Braun was born in France and studied history at Strasbourg University until he decided to pursue his lifelong calling to study the arts. He started out teaching art until he eventually made the leap to full-time illustration.